The Present State of the Congo Question

SPECIALLY
DESIGNED &
PRINTED BY
EDWARD HUGHES
& Co
WELL COURT.
E.C. LONDON. E.C.

Sir ARTHUR CONAN DOYLE
ON THE SITUATION.

The *Daily News* of March 5, contained the following striking letter from Sir ARTHUR CONAN DOYLE :—

To the Editor of the " Daily News.'

Sir,—I read in your issue of March 1st the terrible letter of Mr. D. MacCammond upon the Putomayo rubber trade, and I know well that no word of it is exaggerated. There is only one sentence to which I take exception, and that is " Tribes are held in a bondage that is grimmer and far more dreadful than anything which took place in the Congo." That cannot be true, for nothing which the human imagination could conceive could be more dreadful than the deeds of the Congo, and the roasting of the two small Indian boys which your correspondent cites differs only in being on a smaller scale from a great many incidents which one might narrate.

It would be a thousand pities if the presentation of one great wrong was made the occasion for depreciating or lessening our efforts to remedy another even greater one. Let us by all means bring all possible diplomatic pressure to bear upon the Peruvian Government, and let us do all that the utmost rigour of the British law permits to the erring Company. It is, however, to be borne in mind that though it is a British company in the sense that it is registered in London, it is in truth Peruvian both in its inception, its management, and to an overwhelming extent in its holding of shares. Those British investors who are in the unfortunate position of having put money into it had no possible means of judging from the prospectus what the real nature of the enterprise was or how its working was conducted. So long as they act upon the knowledge now acquired no moral blame can fairly rest upon them.

But the case of the Congo is very different. In Peru we have no direct responsibility. If any outside Power has a direct responsibility it is the United States, which by her Monroe Doctrine, has assumed a position of tutelage over these South American countries. In the Congo, however, the call of duty is clear. We have sworn (in company, it is true, of the other great European Powers) that we would jointly guard the natives. The result of our guardianship has been that in less than thirty years this great country has lost, at a fair computation, about two-thirds of its inhabitants.

An attempt is made now to deal with the subject as if it were concluded. It would be a fatal and inexcusable error if under such a delusion we were to relax our attitude of criticism and to give away our last lever for amelioration by recognising the Belgian annexation. For the moment things are better. But we have no guarantee that they would remain so if the pressure caused by our non-recognition were removed. On the contrary, no one can read the Rev. J. H. Harris's recent letters after his travels through the country without seeing how delusive are the so-called reforms and how threatening the future.

They have given partial free trade, but with such taxes and restrictions upon the trader that it is practically inoperative. They have announced that they will collect taxes in francs instead of in rubber; but as there are no francs in the greater part of the country, they take the equivalent of francs in rubber, arbitrarily fixed, so that the end is much the same. They are starting vast Government plantations and other schemes which can hardly be run save by forced labour. Finally, worst sign of all, they are retaining and restoring many of the old officials, accustomed to outrage and hardened to oppression. If in the face of all these signs we recognise the annexation, it will be to throw away at the last moment all that we have gained during the last ten years of agitation.

I hope that in nothing that I have said I have weakened the case made out by Mr. MacCammond for such action as is possible in the Putomayo district. But it would be a great misfortune if our attention to Peru should in any way relax our vigilance upon the Congo.

ARTHUR CONAN DOYLE.

Grand Hotel, Lyndhurst, New Forest,
March 3.

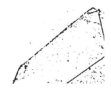

INDEX.

PREFATORY NOTE.

THE concluding phases of a great public movement, when the main object of its promoters has been attained, is perhaps, in a measure, the most trying of all to those immediately concerned.

With no startling facts to place before the Public; with no *active* policy to urge; it is not easy to sustain public interest.

The Congo Reform movement cannot hope to escape the general rule.

Yet the duty of those responsible for the direction of its policy is not entirely fulfilled, and they would be untrue to the cause they have upheld if they remained quiescent at this moment.

A considerable victory has been won, but it is not complete and its results may be jeopardised if the Public do not realise ·—

(1)—That Belgium has given no guarantees that the fundamental reform —the restoration to the Native Communities of their right to the usage of the land and its fruits—which she has introduced into the greater part of the Congo, and promises to apply to the remaining part next July, *has come to stay.*

(2)—That on the contrary Belgium has expressly stated her intention of regarding this reform as *revocable at her will and pleasure.*

(3)—That Belgium still contends, despite clear Treaty stipulations, that the affairs of the Congo are her own concern exclusively.

In Belgium the belief is openly expressed that the British Government will recognise the Annexation in July next, when the third and last portion of the Congo falls under the reform decrees which, as pointed out, are in their essential aspect *revocable.*

Should recognition be granted under those circumstances, all who have interested themselves in this grave problem of national honour and human justice (and who has not?) should clearly understand that the one strong weapon Public Opinion in Britain possesses, to ensure the permanent disappearance of the old wicked system of misrule in the Congo, will have been deliberately thrown away.

There are, doubtless, some who think it expedient to remove the Congo question from the list of international 'controversies, and these tell the Public that whether the conditions be satisfactory or otherwise, " the Belgian Government must be trusted."

That is what is said to the Association.

But it does not meet the case.

While the British Consuls in the Congo themselves report to the British Government that a return to the old evil principles is to be feared, it is still far too soon to ask us to " trust the Belgian Government."

The Belgian Government can, with ease, take such steps as will justify international trust in its intentions and warrant cordial recognition.

For Great Britain to recognise the Belgian annexation until the essential rights of the native population have been permanently secured against any possible return to 'former conditions would be a breach of the national honour as defined by the present Prime Minister of Great Britain, Mr. Asquith, when, at the Guildhall on November 9th, 1909, he declared that this nation has " undertaken solemn obligations towards the native races of the Congo."

The documents published in this Pamphlet embody the statements made above, and illustrate the present position of affairs.

E. D. MOREL.

March, 1912.

ON THE RIGHTS OF THE NATIVES TO DISPOSE IN TRADE OF THE PRODUCTS OF THE SOIL.

GRANVILLE HOUSE,
ARUNDEL STREET, STRAND, LONDON, W.C.
February 19th, 1912.

To the Right Hon. Sir EDWARD GREY, Bart., K.G., P.C.,
His Majesty's Principal Secretary of State for Foreign Affairs,
FOREIGN OFFICE, LONDON.

Sir,

I have the honour, on behalf of the Association, to enclose herewith a letter received by this Association from the Rev. J. H. HARRIS who, as His Majesty's Government are aware, has been travelling extensively in the Congo on behalf of the Anti-Slavery and Aborigines Protection Society.

In forwarding this communication I would venture in the first place to draw the Secretary of State's attention to a fact not without significance.

Although out of direct touch with the Association and ignorant at the time his communication was despatched, of the recent correspondence exchanged between His Majesty's Government and the Association, Mr. HARRIS' estimate of the present situation in the Congo approximates so closely to the views placed by the Association before His Majesty's Government, that the Association's observations and his own might have had a common inspiration.

This is the more interesting since the material upon which the Association founds its views differs altogether from the material at the disposal of Mr. HARRIS.

It will be observed that Mr. HARRIS' fears are—like those of the Association—lest a premature recognition of the Belgian annexation by his Majesty's Government should have consequences disastrous to the objects commonly pursued, _i.e.,_ to the complete and definite freeing of the Congo from those evil principles, with the human misery resulting from them, which have constituted so dark a page in the modern history of Africa.

Mr. HARRIS considers that British recognition next July—which from recent utterances in the Belgian Parliament and Press seems already to be regarded in some quarters in Belgium as a foregone conclusion—would be premature, unless positive guarantees are forthcoming between now and then on certain specific points of vital import to the future of the native races of the Congo.

In this the Association entirely concurs, recognizing, as does Mr. HARRIS, that many salutary changes have been wrought, but realizing, as does Mr. HARRIS, that in important particulars—not so much in the matter of details as in the matter of principles—the situation is insecure and the future outlook by no means reassuring.

In support of his central contention Mr. HARRIS advances three main considerations.

He asks, in the first place, whether the old system has disappeared beyond recall. In that respect he points (a) to the absence of any "recorded guarantee" to that effect ; (b) to the unregulated condition in which the question of native rights in land and in commercial dealing with the land's products still remains ; (c) to the maintenance and to the increasing rise in power and influence of former Congo State Officials, and to the belief openly avowed by these men that the old *régime*, or a *régime* virtually similar will be, and should be, re-introduced.

"It appears to me"—he writes—"as important to obtain for the natives a guarantee of inalienable rights as distinct from privileges both in the land and its natural produce. Whilst such rights remain un-recognised in legislation and in practice, the danger of a Concessionaire System will be a permanent menace to native liberty and international peace."

Without necessarily endorsing, in every particular, the exact form of words used by Mr. HARRIS, the Association is absolutely in accord with his conclusions. This, as the Association has ceaselessly contended—and as it took occasion once more to repeat in its Memorandum to His Majesty's Government of December 5 last—[1] **is the key to the entire situation.**

Until and unless the Native Communities of the Congo are recognized as possessing the inherent right of collecting and disposing in trade of the natural products of their country, their future is wholly insecure.

But that recognition, as the Association has represented to His Majesty's Government from time to time ever since August, 1908—*i.e.*, ever since the Belgian annexation—is withheld by the Belgian Government. In recently published reports His Majesty's Consuls in the Congo pointedly drew attention to the fact. Now Mr. HARRIS does the same.

And His Majesty's Consuls, the Association and Mr. HARRIS agree in looking upon this circumstance, not only as vitiating the entire outlook, but as a presumption that the "sufferance"—to use the expression of Consul MACKIE—now extended to the bulk of the Congo natives to dispose freely of their soil's products, may be at any moment withdrawn and the old state of affairs re-established. A return to the former *régime* of slave-labour in the soil's produce for revenue purposes is, indeed, openly foreshadowed by His Majesty's Consuls.

The question of native rights in disposing in trade of the products of the land is inseparably connected with that of native rights in the land itself. If the former are recognised in legislation and in practice, they automatically involve recognition of the latter, even though satisfactory land legislation be absent. If the former are not recognised, the latter are automatically *nil*, and the Native Communities remain aliens in their own country, deprived of their sole source of advancement, prosperity and progress—indeed, of the fundamental essentials of human liberty.

That is the native side of the case and in the Association's opinion the contention is, and has always been, unanswerable.

---

[1] Document III. in this Pamphlet.

Hence the Association once more makes a pressing appeal to His Majesty's Government, on no account to recognize the Belgian annexation of the Congo until the Belgian Government has furnished explicit guarantees that what is now granted to the Native Communities in the bulk of the Congo (and is to be granted, it is assured, to the remainder next July) on sufferance, shall be recognised as appertaining to them as an intrinsic human right, everywhere admitted as such in tropical Africa, except in the Congo.

What may be described as the European side of the same capital question is referred to by Mr. HARRIS, when he points to the disabilities and injustice under which the European merchant still suffers in the Congo.

On this aspect of the matter His Majesty's Consuls have recently afforded detailed proof and the Association elaborated it at considerable length in the Memorandum submitted to His Majesty's Government in December last. I may now add that the German Congo League, with which the Association preserves harmonious relations, is lately in receipt of similar information which lends weight to the suggestion I made bold to put forward in my letter to His Majesty's Government dated February 5 last.[1] **A principle is here at issue of equal moment to the British and German Governments, both interested in preserving the open door for commerce in Equatorial Africa, both signatories of the Berlin Act, which laid down that freedom of commerce should be an indispensable accompaniment of the privileges conferred by the Powers upon KING LEOPOLD II. and inherited by Belgium.**

The rights of the Native Communities of the Congo to their soil and to their usage of the soil's products for commercial purposes, and the rights of the nationals of the Powers to carry on trade with these Native Communities are inseparable one from the other. Recognition of the former is indispensable to the fulfilment of the latter. There are not two distinct problems at stake, but one problem in a dual aspect.

Mr. HARRIS proceeds to ask whether there are any safeguards that forced labour will not be employed by the Belgian Administration in the matter of the State rubber plantations and other so-called works of public utility. In this

---

1 *Vide (d)* of Document IV. in this Pamphlet.

respect, again, Mr. HARRIS' arguments—and the additional interesting suggestions with which he accompanies them—are, in their essence, a replica of the observations of the Association in the Memorandum to His Majesty's Government in December last.[1] That forced labour is still utilised by the Belgian Administration in all matters affecting public labour for Government is corroborated by Mr. HARRIS. In this important but subsidiary respect, the Belgian Government seems to have made little or no advance since the annexation.

Mr. HARRIS assures us that the feeling prevalent among officials in the Congo is that recognition of annexation by His Majesty's Government will entail a final lapse of all international responsibility for the conditions prevailing in the Congo. This alleged belief does but emphasise the pointed attention drawn in the Association's recent Memorandum to His Majesty's Government to the statement made last October by M. RENKIN, the Belgian Colonial Minister, to Sir FRANCIS VILLIERS, His Majesty's Minister at Brussels[2]—which statement has since formed the subject of correspondence between His Majesty's Government and the Association.

I have the honour to be, Sir,

Your obedient Servant,

(*Signed*) E. D. MOREL,

Hon. Secretary.

---

[1] Document III in this Pamphlet.
[2] *Vide* pages 22 and 23 of this Pamphlet.

COPY of a letter received in February, 1912, from the Rev. J. H. HARRIS, Organising Secretary of the Anti-Slavery and Aborigines Protection Society.

BOMA,

December 30th, 1911.

My dear MOREL,

I have recently received several letters and cuttings which appear to point to the possibility of an early recognition of the transfer of the Congo territory to Belgium. July, 1912, appears to be regarded as the probable date for such recognition, but as these decisions invariably find their genesis much earlier, I think it wise to suggest certain considerations to the members of the Congo Reform Association.

We have now spent many months moving continuously over different areas, covering altogether some thousands of miles, a task which, as you know, has involved us in considerable difficulties, some of which were overcome but others proved insuperable. If, however, there is one thing above another that we can lay claim to, it is that of getting at the back of things amongst the natives themselves, and we are thus enabled to take a general view of the whole situation.

Early Recognition of Annexation to be viewed with "Grave Concern."

We do not wish to say anything which will retard British recognition ; on the contrary, we should greatly rejoice at this taking place, providing satisfaction can be obtained upon several points, but it does seem to us imperative that the Association should weigh certain facts very carefully before acquiescing in such a step on the part of the British Government. At this distance we cannot know the views of the Association, but we are unable to escape from the feeling that had its members spent some months in the Congo, they would view an early recognition with grave concern, unless certain definite guarantees are forthcoming from the Belgian Government.

We are glad to recognise the great change which has come over the Congo, and are prepared to extend an ungrudging, even a warm eulogy to the Belgian

Government, and more especially to King Albert, for the disappearance of certain features of the old *régime*; but there are facts which it would be folly to ignore. These give rise to three questions—

(1)—Is it certain that the old system has disappeared beyond recall?

(2)—Are there any safeguards which preclude the creation of another system of oppression, but little removed from that of former years?

(3)—Will recognition carry with it *in practice* the lapse of those responsibilities and limitations which are imposed by the Conventions and the Acts of the Berlin and Brussels Conferences?

I wish it were possible to give a satisfactory answer to all or to any of these questions, but until we obtain satisfaction upon all three I venture to think recognition would be premature.

I propose dealing briefly with each in turn.

No Guarantee precluding a return to the Old System.

There does not appear to be any recorded guarantee precluding a return in the future of the main features of the old system. The denial of native rights in land is still maintained, no inalienable rights to collect virgin produce has yet been extended to the natives. It is true they collect produce to-day by a sufferance which may be withdrawn at any moment.

Finally, a very large proportion of the old Congo State officials are not only retained but are gradually rising to higher positions and greater influence. These men, in most instances, avow their disbelief in the present condition of affairs, and would, beyond question, welcome the introduction of a *régime* approximating to the old system of commerce allied to administration.

It appears to me as important to obtain for the natives a guarantee of inalienable rights, as distinct from privileges, both in the land and its natural produce. Whilst such rights remain unrecognised in legislation and in practice, the danger of a Concessionaire System will be a perpetual menace to native liberty and international peace.

There is a feature of the old system to which the Belgian Government appears to be firmly wedded, and which, for want of a better term, I must call " Government Commercialism."

Belgian Administration as Merchant.

The Government is the keenest competitor, first in ivory and transport. I have used the word competitor, but in point of fact merchants are not faced with that honourable competition which implies a fair standard of business dealings; they are confronted with a condition of affairs best described in the pugilistic term, "hitting below the belt." In the matter of ivory the Government is guilty of practising every conceivable trick, meanness and illegality in order to obtain "points"[1] from the natives. The tusks, as you know, must be taken to the State to be stamped, and he is a bold native who can successfully resist the pressure to sell at the price the State official offers. The "ten kilo" regulation is another method adopted to secure ivory; very few natives have any but the haziest ideas of weights and measures. Consequently when they carry tusks weighing about ten kilos to be stamped, they frequently find them "confiscated" In the Lomako region the officials adopt a novel plan; a Chief is supplied with guns and ammunition for the express purpose of shooting for ivory for the Government, and this without any respect for the laws of the country as to close season, etc.

If promotion depended upon the ivory obtained by officials they could not be more anxious to obtain " points "; that ivory may be used directly to this end is also possible, for in a large consignment being forwarded to Boma, my attention was drawn to the first "point," a magnificent tusk of over 8 feet, *which was specially packed and addressed by a subordinate, "with compliments," to one of the highest officials in the Service.* It is utterly impossible for merchants to attempt to buy ivory under these conditions, and I suggest that they constitute a clear violation of commercial rights in the Congo.[2]

There is also the question of transport and plantations. It is, of course, a matter for debate whether or not it is wise for a Colonial Government to engage

---

1 *i e* Tusks.—E D. M.
2 See what is said on this matter in the Memorandum to the Foreign Office. Document III.

in such enterprises, but there can be no question as to the evils of this system on the Congo—where by exercise upon the chief of pressure, amounting in some cases to force, which differs little from capture, the Government is able to obtain labour at its own price. Here, again, genuine commercial enterprise has no chance.

It seems to me that the only way to avoid violation of treaties in commercial matters and render the future secure, is to insist upon a separation of the administrative from the trading elements; that was always one of the cardinal features of the British policy as set forth in the speeches of Lord FITZMAURICE.

The State Rubber Plantations.

Granted that public opinion is satisfied that by July, 1912, the old system will have disappeared beyond recall and that recognition should take place, can we be altogether certain that there is no danger of a future development along other lines but little less oppressive than the old Leopoldian *régime*? I have in mind particularly the State Plantations enterprise, concerning the nature of which there seems to be some misunderstanding, for they are compared with those of the British Government on the Gold Coast. The essential difference between them is that those of the British Colonies are experimental, and have, as their object, the assistance of general agricultural development: they are in no sense a commercial venture.[1] Those of the Belgian Government are commercial enterprises of the most extensive order, and bear little, if any, relation to the agricultural development of the Colony. It is true that they are not being extended so rapidly as M. RENKIN's speeches lead the public to believe; it is also true that the existing ones are almost abandoned; but this is due entirely to insufficiency of labour. It is certainly safe to estimate that the labour supply is but one-tenth of the actual requirements and the major part of this is forced labour. Extraordinary stories are floating about as to the means adopted to secure labour. In October I met, ... , who had spent nearly fifteen years of commercial life on the Congo, and, amongst other notes in my diary upon my conversation with him, are the

---

[1] The Gold Coast cocoa plantations are wholly worked by the natives. They belong to the natives, and the industry is, throughout a native one. In Southern Nigeria, the natives have, in many parts, also built up, with the Administration's assistance, communal plantations in rubber.—E. D. M.

following remarks: "Yes, the State frequently calls for 'volunteers' for the Army, and then turns them into workmen on the plantations." . . . . spoke of one occasion when between 200 and 300 were so treated, and added, "They are known as 'volunteers by rope,' that is 'tied by the neck.'"

Works of "Public Utility."

I have visited many of these plantations and certain questions thrust themselves forward on every occasion. "What is M. Renkin waiting for?" and "How does he intend getting labour?" To my mind the answers to both questions are interdependent. M. Renkin knows he can only obtain a sufficiency by the exercise of an extreme measure of force, and that this would cause an uprising of public opinion which would indefinitely postpone British and American recognition. The Belgian Government appears to regard everything it touches as a work of public utility, hence it pleads justification for demanding labour (not, of course, in debates in the Belgian Chamber, but in practice). If profit-bearing enterprises like plantations, transport, wood cutting, are to be classed with roads, bridges and creek clearing, then the day of the abolition of forced labour in the Congo is a long way off. It seems to me essential that some guarantee should be obtained with reference to labour for Government profit-bearing enterprises.

There would be less need for vigilance and caution, if we could rest assured that treaty limitations would be respected, or that there existed in the Colony an independent body of public opinion for the protection of native rights. I have already written to my Committee pointing out that little reliance can be placed upon the existing "Congo Aborigines Protection Commission." Its constitution practically forbids its criticising the Administration adversely, and its composition is such that its knowledge of affairs is very restricted, as witness its amazing ignorance in declaring that food taxes had been abolished.[1]

An Extraordinary View.

I am well aware that in general terms we have been assured that Belgium has always loyally respected treaties, but the language held to British Ministers on

---

[1] That Commission appears to be more interested in theoretical discussions about the relative value of monogamous and polygamous institutions than in anything else.—E.D.M.

several occasions has indicated an extremely novel interpretation of the Convention and Treaties by which the Congo Colony came into existence. You will remember that Sir CHARLES DILKE frequently dwelt upon this as one of the most unsatisfactory features of the Congo question. I have discussed British recognition with a good many Belgians out here, and am surprised to find that they invariably regard British recognition of the transfer as synonymous with the abrogation of Treaties and Conventions. They have frequently expressed the opinion that when "recognition" takes place the Congo territories become the absolute property of Belgium, and all questions by other Governments as to the administration would be sheer impertinence. Indeed, the real desire out here for "recognition" appears to be based solely upon the belief that Belgium will then be freed from awkward questions as to the conduct of the administration.

Such a position would, of course, be untenable in any International Court ; but in view of this opinion so unanimously and firmly held on the spot, coupled with language held to British Ministers, I suggest that it is supremely important to secure most explicit guarantees with reference to Treaty rights and responsibilities, and that the Belgian Government and people should understand clearly that the British nation regards its duty to the Congo natives as one of its most sacred duties towards the so-called subject-races of the world.

In conclusion, I can only reiterate my view that the most explicit guarantees as to the future should precede British recognition of the transfer. This is imperative in the interests of the Congo natives, international harmony, and, in view of certain recent events, to the very existence of Belgium as an independent nation.

Yours sincerely,

(Signed)   JOHN H. HARRIS.

Memorandum

To His Majesty's Government from the Congo Reform Association on the Reports of His Majesty's Consular Staff in the Congo as presented to Parliament, November, 1911.

: *Compiled on behalf of the* ::
CONGO REFORM ASSOCIATION
By E. D. MOREL, Hon. Secretary.
DECEMBER, 1911.

INDEX TO MEMORANDUM.

To the Right Hon. Sir EDWARD GREY, Bart., P.C.; M.P.,
His Majesty's Principal Secretary of State for Foreign Affairs,
FOREIGN OFFICE, LONDON.

December 5th, 1911.

Sir,

I am directed by the Congo Reform Association to acknowledge the receipt of the Secretary of State's letter of November 23rd, from which the Association is glad to note that the points mentioned in my communication of November 13th will be borne in mind when the time comes to consider the question of the British recognition of the annexation of the Congo by Belgium.

I am to state that the Association has observed with much satisfaction from the recent declaration of the Secretary of State in Parliament, that His Majesty's Government are not prepared to consider that question until the whole of the Congo has been released in law from the LEOPOLDIAN system, *i e.,* until July, 1912.

In the view of the Association the Consular Reports now issued by His Majesty's Government, while they happily confirm the existence of improved conditions of the reformed areas, accentuate in the gravest manner many of the fears as to the future which the Association has from time to time expressed.

I have the honour, on behalf of the Association, to attach a Memorandum dealing in considerable detail with the various matters discussed in the Consular Reports, and I am desired to express the hope that His Majesty's Government will give these representations the attention which, it is submitted, the importance of the subject-matter warrants.

Apart from the general analysis of Belgian rule in the Congo according to the Consular Reports (which are discussed in the attached Memorandum), the Association desires me in this communication to lay stress upon two matters which it regards as of capital importance.

The first refers to the maintenance of forced labour—or, more accurately, as Consul ARMSTRONG describes it, " slavery "—imposed by the Belgian Government in the " unreformed " regions of the Congo, in order to raise revenue.

The second refers to the recent utterances of the Belgian Colonial Minister transmitted by Sir FRANCIS VILLIERS.

As to the first matter, the Association deems itself justified in protesting with the utmost vigour against the truly abominable conditions revealed by Consul ARMSTRONG in the " unreformed " regions of the Congo. That the perpetuation of the old system would necessarily be accompanied by the continuance of many of the abuses, which for the past eight years Consul after Consul has reinforced the Association in declaring inseparable from its maintenance, the Association has repeatedly stated; and all its representations to His Majesty's Government in 1907 and 1908 were directed at preventing the system of slavery upheld by King Leopold being reproduced under the Belgian flag. But the protestations of the Belgian Government have been so precise, the belief expressed in them by His Majesty's Government so emphatic, that the Congo Reform Association was not altogether prepared for the picture of systematic wrong-doing, even in the " unreformed " regions, revealed by Consul ARMSTRONG. The Association is not without appreciation of the fact that His Majesty's Government have now published Consul ARMSTRONG's report, but it may, perhaps, be excused for remarking that it does not yet understand why His Majesty's Government should have thought necessary to have withheld that report for ten months.

Setting this aside, the Association would consider it a grave reflection upon British policy that a state of affairs such as that disclosed by Consul ARMSTRONG should be passively acquiesced in by His Majesty's Government for another eight months. The excuse—an excuse containing, in the Association's view, no shadow of validity—put forward by the Belgian Government for so gross an infringement of its duties as a civilised Power in Africa, is deprived by the recent judicial decision in the matter of the " Crown Domain " moneys, of all *raison d'être*. The Belgian Government now has at its disposal a sum of £2,000,000; more than ten times sufficient to replace the revenue which would be lost by an immediate cessation of this system of slavery in the " unreformed " regions (and also to lower the onerous incidence of taxation in the " reformed " regions). For the Belgian Government, under these circumstances, to persist in such wrong-doing for the best part of another year, would be to exceed in scandalous disregard of civilised obligations and duties all previous performances of the Congo.

As to the second matter, the Association directs me to draw pointed attention to the closing words of the last Despatch printed in the White Book—the Despatch dated October 27th last from Sir FRANCIS VILLIERS, the new British Minister at Brussels. Referring to a conversation held on March 8th last between Sir ARTHUR HARDINGE, His Majesty's late Minister at Brussels, and M. RENKIN, the Belgian Colonial Minister, Sir FRANCIS VILLIERS transmits to His Majesty's Government the Belgian Colonial Minister's views of the significance properly attaching to that conversation. It was regarded by the Belgian Colonial Minister, Sir FRANCIS VILLIERS states, as quite "unofficial," since the matter discussed (*i.e.*, Consul ARMSTRONG Report) "was one which exclusively concerned the internal administration of a Belgian Colony."

To this pretension, viz., that the affairs of the Congo State are a matter of exclusive Belgian concern, the Association takes the strongest possible exception, and ventures to believe that His Majesty's Government will not have failed to have pointed out to the new British Minister at Brussels that it is a pretension which His Majesty's Government can in no way recognise.

The subject is, in the view of the Association, of such paramount importance that I make bold to recall the correspondence in connection with similar pretensions on the part of the Belgian Colonial Minister, which has passed between His Majesty's Government and the Congo Reform Association, especially in April and May of last year.[1]

The Association is strongly of opinion that this persistency on the part of the Belgian Government in denying the right of other Powers signatory to the Berlin Act to criticise, and if necessary to intervene, in the affairs of the Congo State so long as the administration of the Congo State continues to be conducted in a manner contrary to the terms of that Act, calls for a clear and explicit repudiation on the part of His Majesty's Government. M. RENKIN's reiterated declaration challenges, in effect, the position of His Majesty's Government under Treaty, and were that challenge allowed to pass unnoticed, public misapprehension as to the rights and obligations of this country could not fail, it is submitted, to arise both at home and abroad.

The Association ventures to hope that in addition to instructions which may have been transmitted to His Majesty's Minister at Brussels on the subject, His Majesty's Government may also find it possible to reassure the public mind in this country on the point.

I have the honour to be, Sir,

Your obedient Servant,

E. D. MOREL,

Hon. Secretary.

---

[1] *a* (From the Congo Reform Association, April 10, 1910.)
b (From the Foreign Office, May 10, 1910)
c (From the Congo Reform Association, May 12, 1910.)

Memorandum on the Reports of His Majesty's Consular Staff on the Congo, 1910-1911 (Africa No. 2, 1911).

—————o>o<o————

The observations I am desired to submit to His Majesty's Government in connection with the Consular Reports now issued will be found to be divided into Sections as follows :—

SECTION I.—Present conditions of the Natives in the Areas where the Reform Decrees have been applied.

SECTION II.—Present condition of the Natives in the Areas where the Reform Decrees have not been applied.

SECTION III.—The Future Outlook.

SECTION III. will be found to be sub-divided as follows :—

(a) The Permanence of Reform.

(b) The Prospects of Trade Development.

(c) The Government Rubber Plantations : Forced labour for works of " Public Utility ": The Native Army.

PREFATORY REMARKS.

A majority in the Belgian Chamber of 29 in a House of 166 Members (of whom only 83, or one-half, voted in favour) decided in August, 1908, to annex the Congo State on terms ensuring for further long periods a continuation of the abuses and illegalities of the old system.

The Belgian Annexation and the policy of the Congo Reform Association.
The Congo Reform Association had from the first supported the policy of a Belgian annexation as the most practicable means of suppressing the evils prevailing in the Congo State.

But only on the understanding that annexation should *coincide* with the radical suppression of the operative causes of these admitted evils, the operative causes being :—

(a)—The claim of the Congo State Government to the negotiable wealth of the land, thus depriving the native population of all right to collect the natural products of the soil and to dispose of them in trade.

(b)—The compulsion exercised by the Congo State Government upon the native population to force the latter to collect these natural products as a "tax," from the proceeds of which the Congo State Government obtained its revenue.

The above system of rule imposed by the Congo State had been repeatedly denounced by the Unionist and Liberal Governments of Great Britain as "slavery," so far as its effects upon the native population were concerned, and as a violation of the commercial clauses of the Berlin Act so far as its effects upon Afro-European trade in the Congo were concerned.

Consequently the Association considered that the *prima facie* requirement of any scheme of annexation of the Congo by Belgium was the extraction of binding guarantees from the Belgian Government that this system of slavery and illegality would be abrogated *concurrently with annexation.* This view was held by an influential section of the party in Belgium which desired annexation, but an annexation of the same character as that urged by the Association.

The Association has seen no cause to alter its view that annexation of this character could have been secured—to the great good both of the Congo and of Belgium—had His Majesty's Government adhered to the position they took up in November, 1906, and on February 26, 1908 ; and the Association has not had occasion to regret that it pressed that view steadily upon His Majesty's Government for two years.

After the annexation vote in August, 1908, the old system remained in force all over the Congo under the Belgian flag until July 1, 1910, when by the Reform Scheme of November, 1909, subsequently confirmed by the Royal Decree of March 22, 1910, the system was abolished (with reservations)[1] by law in one section of the territory. In July, 1911, it was abolished (with reservations)[1] by law in another section of the territory. It is still in force in certain regions, *i.e., three years after annexation the Belgian Government is still obtaining revenue by slavery and illegality in a portion of the Congo State territory.*

See Section III A., paragraphs X. and XI.

SECTION I.

Present condition of the Natives in the Areas where the Reform Decrees have been applied.

I.   The conditions prevailing in the portions of the territory where the old system is, by law, abolished (with reservations)[1] are discussed in despatches from Vice-Consul THURSTAN August 25, 1910)), Acting-Consul CAMPBELL (October 25, 1910), Vice-Consul THURSTAN (December 31, 1910) Consul MACKIE (May 30, June 2, June 26, 1911).   These reports indicate a marked improvement in former conditions, which, indeed, was bound to follow from the abolition of the old system.

The Association notes with satisfaction the beginning of methods approximating to civilised rule.[2]   It regrets to be unable to describe its satisfaction as unreserved, in view of several causes giving rise to anxiety for the future as indicated in Section III. of this Memorandum.

Apart from these general causes inviting justifiable apprehension, the Association desires to call attention to three points mentioned by the Consular Staff as involving maladministration and hardship, viz.:

(a)—The retention in the service of the Belgian Government of officials compromised by the old system.

(b)—The retention in positions of authority over native communities of upstarts (sometimes ex-soldiers) invested with no hereditary claim to the Chieftainship.

(c)—The difficulty which natives experience in certain districts to pay their taxes in silver coin, owing to the absence or insufficiency of that medium.

The Taxes in Silver. Coin.

II.   The latter point is referred to in Section III. in connection with trade development; but it may be here remarked that a direct tax in silver coinage levied upon a primitive people may in certain circumstances prove as great, indeed a greater, hardship than a *definitely regulated* tax in produce.   Under the new system, practically every adult male is assessed at an annual tax which varies from four-and-twopence to ten shillings—payable in coin.   In the first place the average mean of this taxation is very much higher than that prevailing in

---

1 See Section IIIA Paragraphs X & XI.
2 See Section IIIA. Paragraph IX.

other tropical African dependencies, expressed in terms of actual cash. When the impoverishment and exhaustion of the Congo—constantly accentuated by the British Consular Staff—is taken into account, the ratio of taxation is enormously higher than that prevailing in other tropical dependencies. Moreover, the Consuls bear witness all through these reports to the difficulty experienced by the natives inhabiting the remoter districts in obtaining silver coinage at all.[1] To demand of a native community that possesses no markets in which to dispose of its saleable commodities, or which possesses no saleable commodities to dispose of even if it had markets (and both cases are cited by the Consuls), and which is unable, therefore, to obtain silver tokens in the ordinary process of trade, is tantamount to forcing that native community into slavery or driving it into armed rebellion. The imposition of a direct tax in silver coin upon a primitive people is, in principle, only justifiable where that people is in a position to acquire it through the medium of commercial transactions, and of the immense majority of the natives of the Congo it may be truly said that they are not yet in that position.

The incidence of the Tax. III. Eliminating the population of the unreformed region (in order not to confuse the argument now advanced), as given in CONSUL CAMPBELL'S tables,[2] the total estimated population of the reformed region of the Congo is reckoned at just over six millions—men, women and children. In another table the total estimated *taxable* population of the *whole* Congo is given at 2,007,087, or 1,671,809, deducting the taxable population of the unreformed regions.[3] But this taxable population includes men and women, women, as a foot-note indicates, being no longer taxable. Hence at the very outside estimate, the taxable population of the reformed regions of the Congo (*i.e.*, the regions where a tax in silver coin is imposed) is to-day half that total, viz., 835,904, or, in round numbers, 840,000. Now the Belgian Government reckons to obtain from these supposititious 840,000 male adults next year in taxes, no less than 7,150,000 francs paid in silver coin.[4] In other words, even on this basis of calculation, which is largely favourable to the Belgian Government, the incidence of taxation works out at the rate of over 8 francs per head imposed upon an exhausted and impoverished people. A tax in silver, even unjustifiably heavy, is so immeasurably an improvement over an unregulated so-called "tax" in produce, which involved the tax-payer in continuous labour all the year, that the change may well have come as a comparative blessing. But one may safely predict that the present excessive incidence will, if maintained, prove to be an intolerable burden. It may be reiterated that nowhere in Africa are primitive communities of forest-dwellers taxed so heavily by their European overlords.

---

1 Confirmed to the Association by the American Missionaries in the Kasai.
2 pp 16 and 17 of the White Book.
3 Numbering 335,278 (White Book).
4 *Vide* Budget des recettes et des dépenses du Congo belge, pour l'exercice (p. 57).

SECTION II.

Present Condition of the Natives in the Areas where the Reform Decrees have not been applied.

Continued Abuses. IV. The state of affairs in the unopened regions is extremely grave and unhappily bears out the predictions of the Association as to the situation which could not fail to persist if the Belgian Government were permitted to annex the Congo on the basis of the old system.

Consul ARMSTRONG's report is, indeed, very nearly as bad as any intelligence which has been received from the Congo, even in the worst days of the old *régime*. It conveys the clearest proof that the Belgian Government is maintaining in the unreformed regions, the same atrociously cruel and destructive form of slavery which has been responsible for the depopulation and economic exhaustion of the past twenty years.

Staggering Depopulation. V. The extent of that depopulation is now rendered evident for the first time officially. It can only be described as appalling.

That STANLEY's original estimate of the population of the Congo at forty-three millions, made a quarter of a century ago, was exaggerated is doubtless true. But at the time of the annexation of the Congo by Belgium, the Belgian Government asserted that the population was anything between thirty and twenty millions. Consul CAMPBELL now produces information gathered from local official sources which gives the estimated total population at only 7,248,000 !

The following table possesses an eloquence which needs no emphasising:—

	Total area in square miles,	Total population,
British Dependencies in } [1] Tropical Africa .... }	928,535	26,026,790
German Dependencies in } [2] Tropical Africa .... , .. }	574,209	12,000,000
The Congo State	900,000	7,248,303

The "unreformed" areas are the only ones in the Congo to which to-day the terms "densely populated" can apply. They contain more than one-seventh of the entire remaining population.[3] *Yet it is these very regions which the*

---

[1] Nyassaland, Uganda, British East Africa, Northern Nigeria, Southern Nigeria, Gold Coast, Sierra Leone, Gambia.
[2] German East Africa and Cameroons, (excluding Territory recently acquired from France).
[3] 1,189,000 (p. 17). (White Book).

Belgian Government has been subjecting since the annexation in August, 1908, to the process of systematic bleeding (which has resulted in such disaster to the other parts of this unhappy territory) until they, too, will be reduced to the same condition of physical and economic exhaustion, as plainly foreshadowed by Consuls Armstrong and Campbell.

VI. We feel that we cannot adequately comment upon the crushing indictment contained in Consul ARMSTRONG'S report, confirmed as it is in a general way by Consul-General MACKIE.[1] That such a state of affairs—"a direct system of slavery created and maintained by the Government," as Consul ARMSTRONG puts it—should still prevail in a region of Africa, for the welfare of whose inhabitants the civilised Powers undertook solemn responsibilities, is the bitterest satire upon the morality of Governments. That it should be enforced by the Power which, boasting of its wealth and industry, declared when it annexed the Congo that one of its "loftiest preoccupations" was the fulfilment of the "civilising mission" it had undertaken,[2] will, the Association feels, bring its own inevitable punishment.

The Belgian Government's illegal traffic in arms and the International dangers arising therefrom. There is, however, one aspect of the Belgian Government's misrule in the unreformed regions as to which, it would seem, the direct interest of His Majesty's Government can be appealed to, apart from obligations of honour involved in His Majesty's Government's frequent admissions of responsibility towards the native races of the Congo. It is one that the Association has frequently referred to and which has formed the subject of questions in the House of Commons influenced by the Association. We refer to the traffic in arms carried on by the Belgian Government in order to procure ivory and rubber for purposes of revenue, in defiance of International Conventions. This charge is now brought with all the weight properly attaching to a Report of one of His Majesty's Consuls, for the accuracy of which His Majesty's Government, in publishing it, assumes responsibility. Consul ARMSTRONG, we observe, declares that the sale of arms and ammunition by the Belgian Government has reached in the Uele district "the most alarming proportions." The greater part of these arms, he says, "have been given in exchange for ivory." The violation of the Arms and Ammunition Conference is complete. "Nearly all the freemen in every village have guns." "Chiefs have as many as 150." They all appear to possess "unlimited quantities of powder and caps." The fatuity of the proceeding even from the point of view of the Belgian Government's own ultimate interest is shown by the fact that "in order to counteract the effect of distributing large quantities of arms and ammunition, a force of considerably over 1,000 troops is distributed over the Uele district." The situation is thus summarised by Consul ARMSTRONG:

" And while this matter would be solely the business of the Government were there no other colonies touching on the borders of the Uele district, in effect a great deal of trade in guns and ammunition is actually carried on between the Congo and the neighbouring colonies. That this state of affairs is highly dangerous is manifest. The relations between the Congo Government and some of its chiefs on the north of the Uele River are almost hostile. And everything points to an uprise in the near future. I have pointed this out elsewhere in this report showing that such a situation has arisen as the result of investing chiefs with despotic rights over the people in order to enforce rubber and other taxes. And these chiefs being obliged to resort to the most abusive means in order to enforce the payment of taxes are given numbers of guns to protect themselves against the vengeance of their people. At regular intervals therefore they have been obliged to listen to the demands of their people, and thus defy the Government. This state of affairs has been going on for years. Chiefs who are the Government's friends to-day are its enemies to-morrow. To supply them with guns and ammunition therefore is to invite them to revolt whenever the occasion presents itself. There is scarcely a chief in the Uele district who has not at some time or other been forced into this situation. Punitive expeditions have been sent against them, which have resulted in the reinstatement of the chiefs and the re-establishment of the rubber tax. This state of affairs can be seen in almost all its evolutionary stages at the present time, and would therefore appear to be almost a direct line of policy."

A more disgraceful state of affairs it would be difficult to imagine.

VII. The Association cannot but record its surprise that in the Despatch addressed to Sir A. HARDINGE by the Secretary of State on March 3, 1911, commenting upon Consul ARMSTRONG's Report, as in the reported conversation between the Belgian Colonial Minister and Sir A. HARDINGE following upon that Despatch, no mention appears to have been made of this traffic in arms on the part of the Belgian Government, described by Consul ARMSTRONG as "a positive menace to the tranquillity, not only of the Belgian Colony, but also of the neighbouring Colonies."

SECTION III.

THE FUTURE OUTLOOK.

A.—The Permanence of Reform.

VIII. In presenting to the Government its observations on the future outlook, the Association desires to base itself solely upon what are admitted facts, and to confine itself more particularly to such of these admitted facts as possess capital importance in determining the problem of the future of Belgian Rule on the Congo.

Satisfactory features in the Budgetary Estimates for 1912. The fact most pregnant of promise is to be sought, in the Association's view, rather in the budgetary estimates for 1912 than in the pages of the White Book. The salient points in the Belgian Parliamentary Paper (No. 5) giving the estimated revenue and expenditure returns for 1912, are as follows :

Estimated receipts — ... — —	£1,814,705.
Estimated ordinary expenditure —	£1,988,812.
Estimated extraordinary expenditure .... —	£672,746.

These figures show an estimated loss for the year's working of £174,107 and an estimated sum of £672,746 to be, in part, invested by Belgium in the Congo in the shape of capital expenditure next year. The significance of the figures lies in this, that, as a consequence of the reforms already introduced and foreshadowed, and of the general change in governing ideas, Belgium will be spending next year in connection with the Congo the sum of £846,853. That any attempt to retrieve the Congo from the morass of misery and economic ruin into which the Leopoldian System had plunged it, would of necessity involve its new governors in heavy expenditure, of which the present sum can in the nature of the case only be a very small instalment, was, of course, obvious. It is also unhappily true that the greater part of the "extraordinary" expenses are not devoted to objects calculated to relieve the native population of the Congo of the burden of taxation resting upon it. On this point indeed many reserves would require to be made. Nevertheless the Association feels that this first proof that Belgium has realised the truth that the Congo can no longer be treated as a milch-cow is so important as to warrant the Association in laying great stress upon it.

A feature in the revenue estimates is the estimated fall in the revenues derived from the rubber and ivory "taxes" of £298,976. This fall is to a certain extent counterbalanced by the increased receipts under taxes in silver coin. Some of the injustices the latter involve, as at present imposed, and the dangers to be apprehended from their continuance at the present ratio of incidence, has already been touched upon.[1]

Satisfactory features in the Consular Reports. IX.—Accompanied as they are by sundry warnings and grave criticism, the Consuls' reports in so far as they deal with the reformed areas are encouraging, and the opinions of a number of missionaries therein quoted the Association rejoices to note. There can be no doubt that the *present* situation in the reformed areas is altogether different from what it was, and the Association is the less likely to wish to minimise these improvements, since it is able with some justice to claim that its own labours have not been foreign to securing them. But the word "present" needs to be accentuated because when, turning from a contemplation of the present as compared with the dreadful past, the Consuls look into the future, they hardly make a pretence of concealing their anxiety. This anxiety the Association shares, and the main causes of it will now be indicated.

Unsatisfactory character of the Decree restoring to the Natives the right to trade. X.—In numerous preceding communications, and again in the action taken by the Executive Committee of the Congo Reform Association on November 7 (duly communicated to His Majesty's Government and acknowledged by them),[2] the Association has emphasised the unsatisfactory character of the Royal Decree of March, 1910, in so far as it appeared by its very wording to cast doubt upon the permanence of the capital reform therein announced—and since applied in the 1910 and 1911 areas—*i.e*, the restoration to the native population of its right to collect the natural products of the soil and dispose of them in trade. The Association believes it can assert without fear of contradiction that His Majesty's Government fully share its view as to the paramount importance of this reform. Indeed, it is safe to say that there is an absolute concensus of opinion on the subject in all quarters. No change in the conditions of the Congo can be lasting which does not guarantee to the native population *for all time* its right to buy and to sell. And it is here precisely that the Reform Decrees give rise to serious doubts as to the Belgian Government's intentions.

---

[1] *Vide* Section I Paragraph III.
[2] Letter from the Congo Reform Association to the Foreign Office, Nov. 13, 1911, acknowledged Nov. 23, 1911.

Uncertain position of the Natives.

XI. In allowing it to be inferred that a return to the *status quo ante* is possible, that this restoration of an elementary human right to the native population is not the acknowledgment in equity and law of such right, but merely a revocable concession, the Belgian Government at once invites and compels suspicion. That suspicion can only be intensified by the circumstance that, concurrently, the Belgian Government has taken no legislative step calculated to modify the old Leopoldian conception of land, which, without in anyway defining the word " State," declared—to quote the words used by His Majesty's Government—"all lands State property regardless of native rights."[1] On this particular point the Association can add nothing to the document it presented to His Majesty's Government at the close of 1908, in acknowledging which the Foreign Secretary was good enough to say that " the exhaustive and closely-reasoned memorandum enclosed will be of great assistance to His Majesty's Government in their efforts to secure the restoration to the natives of their rights." If the restoration to the natives of their rights to deal freely in the *produce of the land* were made absolute, the absence of legislation recognising native communal rights in *the land itself*, might well be left unpressed, since, in a practical sense, the question would be solved thereby. But so long as any doubt remains as to the permanent character of this restoration, the absence of legislation recognising native tenure assumes extreme significance. *The Association most earnestly appeals to His Majesty's Government not to leave this question in the state it now is.* No assurances from Belgium, however eloquent, are worth the paper upon which they are written if the guarantee of permanence to this restoration of native right in the free collection and disposal of natural products is lacking. The gravity of the question is strikingly illustrated in the Consuls' reports, in numerous passages which bear directly or indirectly upon it. We find Consul CAMPBELL drawing attention to the absence of recognition of native rights in the land[2] and to the power invested in the Governor-General to suspend the right of collecting its products.[3] Elsewhere the Consul openly foreshadows the possibilities of a return " to the old *régime*."[4] Consul ARMSTRONG, in pointing "to the fact that the Government intends to make free trade as difficult as possible," conveys a similar warning.[5] Consul MACKIE describes rightly, and in accordance with the Decree of March, 1910, the present enjoyment on the part of the natives of gathering produce for trade as " still a simple sufferance."[6] " A reversion to the old system " is discussed as a possibility in the same report.[7]

1 Memorandum annexed to Despatch, November 4, 1908.
2 p. 2. of the White Book.
3 pp 4 and 5 of the White Book.
4 p. 12. of the White Book.
5 p. 26. of the White Book.
6 p. 53. of the White Book.
7 p. 86. of the White Book.

B.—The Prospects of Trade Development.

The Connection between Native Rights and European Commerce.

XII. Intimately bound up with the question of this inherent right of the native to trade, *i.e.*, to indulge in commercial activity, which lies at the root of human freedom, is the question whether the native is or is not to have *the opportunity of putting that right into actual practice.* He can only exercise it if he is supplied with markets. He can only be supplied with markets so far as his trade relations with the outer world are concerned, through the European merchant. The problem on its European side is, therefore, intimately bound up with its African side. The two, indeed, cannot be separated. The European Governments. are by Treaty empowered to secure for their nationals, liberty to trade with the native peoples of the Congo. But this liberty becomes inoperative in practice if the native peoples of the Congo are not free to collect and dispose of their produce in trade with Europeans. Consequently the first condition the European Governments are required to ensure is that the natives of the Congo shall be recognised as possessing the incontestible right to deal in commerce with Europeans, which they, can only do through the collection and sale of natural products. This requirement is not fulfilled in a satisfactory manner so long as the natives of the Congo are permitted to do so merely "on sufferance."[1] The second condition is that trade between Europeans and Natives shall not be so hampered and restricted as to injure its development. Here again the inherent rights of the native peoples of the Congo, coincide with the legitimate commercial rights of Europeans. There can be no trade without merchants. If the Belgian Government makes impossible conditions for the merchant, commerce cannot hope to gain a permanent footing in the Congo, and the way will be left open, this time through another avenue, for a return to the old *régime*. The salvation of the Congo peoples depends upon the development of commerce.

Obstacles to Trade Development.

XIII. It is impossible, the Association thinks, to peruse the White Book the Government has now laid before Parliament without feeling that this danger is a very real one, and that the development of trade relations[2] between the native peoples of the Congo and the outer world is seriously threatened from two sides. First, through the onerous taxes levied upon trade. Secondly, through the further foreshadowed demands upon native labour by the Belgian Government. The first danger is an actual one. The second is a potential one, although clearly indicated. We now crave permission to deal with the first of these dangers.

---

1 Apart from the self-evident unsatisfactoriness of the Decree of March, 1910, Consul CAMPBELL's remark on page 12 of the White Book, where he says that by the end of July traders "can be *more or less certain* that the rubber which they purchase will not be seized," is highly significant.

2 The Association regrets the confusion which the words "free trade" give rise to in many minds. If for "free trade" the words "freedom of trade" were substituted in dealing with this matter, the idea so frequently entertained that the problem is any way connected with controversies affecting "free trade" and differential tariffs would be removed.

The Three Articles in which Commercial Transactions are possible.
XIV. The three articles which possess sufficient intrinsic value to pay for export to Europe from the Upper Congo (*i.e.* from four-fifths of the territory) the only articles, therefore, in which commercial transactions are possible at present, and probably for many years to come, are rubber, ivory and gum copal. The Consular Reports add little to our knowledge of the conditions under which the gum copal trade can be carried on. On the other hand, they are replete with voluminous details concerning the conditions of trade in rubber and in ivory.

Handicaps placed upon the Rubber Trade.
XV. With regard to rubber, Consul CAMPBELL, we observe, while admitting that the reduction in taxes is "comparatively generous," allows that even in this revised form they are still "heavy." However, he appears on the whole to regard the changes in the light of "advantages" by comparison with the earlier taxes imposed by the Belgian Administration. He illustrates his conclusion by a comparative table. This table[1] consists (a) of the list of taxes drawn up by Herr VOHSEN published in the *Berliner Tageblatt* and brought to the attention of His Majesty's Government in the Memorial from this Association of November 1909[2] designed to show what a European merchant acquiring $1\frac{1}{4}$ *hectares* of land in a rubber-producing district, building thereon a trade *depôt* and exporting on his own steamer 20 tons of rubber *per annum*, would have to pay to the Belgian Government in fees and taxes; (b) a list of fees and taxes which a European merchant under similar circumstances would have to pay to the Belgian Government under the revised scale. But a comparison of the old and new taxes, as shown in this table, do not appear to bear out the Consul's views as to the latter constituting an advantage over the former. Herr VOHSEN showed that the European merchant would have to pay :—

(1) a lump sum of 5,000 francs ; (2) a yearly sum of 32,017.50 francs.

The Consul shows that the European merchant will have to pay :—

(a) an annual lump sum of 250 francs ; (b) a yearly sum of 40,357.50 francs.

These totals may be compared thus :—

Old system of handicapping trade :	New system of handicapping trade :
Lump sum (not recurring) to be paid by merchant £200	Recurring annual lump sum to be paid by merchant £10
Annual payments by merchant £1,280	Annual payments by merchant ...£1,614

---

1 pp 6 & 7 of the White Book.
2 An analysis and criticism of the Belgian Government's proposals.

The merchant in a worse position than ever.

XVI. The net result, therefore, would seem to be that the European merchant is in a worse position than ever. It would interest the Association very much to know whether His Majesty's Government associate themselves with the Consul in deducing from these figures, that the new arrangement constitutes an "advantage" to the European merchant. The situation works out thus. The European merchant desirous of opening up a trade in rubber in the Congo is called upon to pay to the Belgian Government in fees, licenses, export duties and taxes of various kinds, more than 2 francs per *kilo*. When this is added to the price paid to the native for the article itself (which must, as the Consul rightly points out, rise with competition) and the merchant's own expenses of up-keep, wages, handling and transport in the Congo to port of ocean shipment, freight to Europe, warehouse charges and brokers' fees, etc., at port of discharge, one is almost forced to the conclusion that at the back of the Belgian Government's mind there must be either gross ignorance of local conditions, or a desire not to encourage, but on the contrary to hamper trade. Certainly in no part of Africa outside the Congo Basin is trade handicapped by such preposterous charges, and yet in no part of Africa do circumstances so imperatively demand that international trade should be assisted in every way possible by generous treatment. The situation is aggravated by the fact that the merchant is further handicapped as a rubber exporter by the unfair competition, as an exporter, of the very Government which makes these charges upon his business. We refer to this matter at greater length under the Section headed "State Rubber Plantations."

What are the Belgian Government's motives in hampering Trade Development?

XVII. The Consuls do not conceal their own suspicion of what the Belgian Government's intentions may be. Attention has already been drawn to some of their utterances in the paragraph dealing with the natives' right to trade at all. But the Consuls are just as emphatic when they refer to the policy of the Belgian Government in hindering Europeans from trading with the natives. In this connection there is a remarkable passage in Consul ARMSTRONG's Report[1] in which he makes the astonishing statement that in the reformed areas Belgian Officials are offering up to 3 francs per *kilo* to the natives for rubber "in order to protect the natives against a possible combination among merchants to keep down the price of rubber." Considering that the Belgian Officials, as the Consul gives ample proof, are *forcing* the natives in the unreformed areas to bring them rubber for a nominal 2½d. a *kilo* (*which actually works out, as the Consul shows, at 6½ ounces of salt for one month's work, and a fathom of cloth value 1s. 4d. for six months' work*), it is not easy to credit the Belgian Government with disinterested zeal for the welfare of the inhabitants of the Congo. But that the Belgian Government should

---

[1] p. 96 of the White Book.

be buying, or offering to buy, rubber in the reformed areas at all is a surprising revelation, and opens up quite a new vista of future complications. Consul ARMSTRONG goes on to say that while the *Belgian Government is forcing rubber out of the natives at a nominal 2½d. per kilo in the unreformed areas*, the natives in the reformed areas nowhere get less than 2 francs (1s. 8d.) from European merchants. Why, then, is the Belgian Government attempting to make the merchants force up their price? Is it with the idea of assisting the natives? The Belgian Government's action in the unreformed areas provides the best answer to that. Is it, on the other hand, with the idea of making trade impossible, and so provide an excuse for the return to the *status quo ante*, the old system of violence and slavery (still upheld by the Belgian Government in the unreformed area) over the whole territory? Consul ARMSTRONG appears to entertain no doubts on the subject. He recalls the " increased duties on rubber, to which must be added the enormous transport charges," and says that for the Belgian Government to insist upon merchants paying " a minimum price of 3 francs per *kilo* may prove more than the prices in Europe will permit." In other words it may kill the nascent trade which is replacing the old *régime*. The Consul concludes :

> "All the evidence, then, points to the fact that the Government intends to make free trade as difficult as possible. And merchants who foresee in this policy a scheme by which the Government seeks to hinder the expansion of private enterprise in the areas opened to free trade in July, 1910, and thus eventually to substitute a monopoly as existed heretofore, cannot be blamed for showing a lack of confidence in Government assurances "

Consul MACKIE reports[1] a conversation with the Vice-Governor General in which the latter expressed his disappointment " that traders had been slow to avail themselves of the trading opportunities offered to them in the districts opened to free trade." The wonder is that any merchants should have had the courage to enter the reformed areas at all under circumstances so utterly discouraging.

Handicaps placed upon the Ivory Trade.
XVIII. It is difficult to gather from the Consuls' reports what are the exact conditions prevailing at the moment in the reformed areas with regard to the trade in ivory. Certain passages in some of the reports appear to indicate that the old system of demanding as a " tax," either from the buyers (*i.e.* the merchant) or from the vendor (*i.e.* the native) *one half the quantity of ivory forming the object of the transaction*, remains in force.[2] Other passages elsewhere suggest that this iniquitous system has been aggravated by a new law virtually prohibiting the export of any ivory at all, except by the Government.[3] Merchants, Consul CAMPBELL asserts, are liable to have their ivory " seized at any moment." He instances the case of one firm having

---

[1] p. 77 of the White Book
[2] *Arrêts* of 1889 and 1905
[3] p. 10 of the White Book.

202 points of ivory seized; of another mulcted in 55 points, and so on. Whatever the precise state of the law may be, all the reports agree as to the general position. Consul CAMPBELL declares that the law " practically closes the Congo to ivory traders." Consul ARMSTRONG is equally emphatic, so is Consul THURSTAN.[1]

In the unreformed areas the Belgian Government continues to acquire ivory for revenue purposes, partly by force, partly in exchange for guns and ammunition? at fabulous profits, judging from Consul ARMSTRONG's statements, i.e. *a cap gun worth 4/- in Europe and priced at £1. 4s. in the Uelle for 180 to 200 kilograms of ivory worth £180 to £200.*

Trade Development stifled. **XIX.** Thus the Belgian Government would seem to aim at making trade in the two most important articles of commerce in the Congo a virtual impossibility, except (so far as rubber is concerned) in the Kasai, where the powerful Kasai Company, though not now possessed of a monopoly in law, enjoys a virtual monopoly in practice, based, in part at least, upon the method of paying a powerful native chief, employing armed guards, " a substantial commission per ton on all the rubber collected in his country . . . .,"[3] " with one object, that of indirectly fostering the rubber production."[4]

C.—The Government Rubber Plantations : Forced Labour for Works of Public Utility: The Native Army.

Are future demands to be made upon Native Labour by the Belgian Government? **XX.** The *inherent right* of the native peoples of the Congo to trade in the produce of their soil, as that right is affected by the Decree of March, 1910; and the *opportunity afforded to them of so doing*, as affected by the conditions under which European merchants are able to conduct commercial operations in the country; have both been examined. We have seen that in these respects the economic liberty (and consequently the human freedom) of these peoples is not secure under the existing policy of the Belgian Government. The position of the natives—as revealed by the White Book—in that respect, has now to be discussed from the point of view of the Belgian Government's demands upon native labour. It is obvious that if, upon the obstacles already prevalent as regards the free development of trade, there is to be grafted the additional obstacle of incessant demands for labour for " public" purposes (or purposes so represented) the future of the native peoples of the Congo becomes increasingly hazardous. That such danger is to be apprehended cannot—the Association fears—be contested.

---

1 p. 38 of the White Book.
2 *Vide* Section II , par VI.
3 Consul THURSTAN p. 45 of the White Book
4 id. p. 46 of the White Book (Consul THURSTAN, the Association is glad to note, reports a great lessening in the hardships of the natives in connection with the rubber exploitation in the Kasai. But that, of course is not the point specially dealt with in this section of the Memorandum).

Mr. Asquith and Great Britain's "solemn obligations" towards the Native Peoples of the Congo.

XXI. Before dealing specifically with the direction whence this danger is to be chiefly dreaded, the Association may be permitted to recall Mr. ASQUITH's utterances at the Guildhall on November 9, 1909, in the relation they bear to the Reports of His Majesty's Consuls in the White Book. Speaking of the Congo Reform movement in this country the Prime Minister said:—

"It is disinterested; it is sincere; it has no ulterior or selfish motive. It is in no sense impertinent, for it has regard to a territory and a population towards which by treaty we have undertaken solemn obligations."

What is the condition to-day of this population towards which Great Britain has "undertaken solemn obligations," as described by the British Consular staff? It is one of great exhaustion following upon twenty years of brutal violence, unrelieved tyranny, barbarous and destructive despotism, which are now seen to have reduced the number of inhabitants of the Congo basin to an extent exceeding the gloomiest speculations of the most fervent upholder of Congo reform.[1] The "solemn obligations," of this country, and of Europe generally, towards the Congo peoples have been singularly inefficacious in preventing those peoples from being decimated in a manner which can hardly be paralleled in history. The remnant is wearied, morose, impoverished. Disease sweeps its ranks. The economic resources of the land have, in many cases, temporarily, at any rate, disappeared.

Consuls' statements as to Exhaustion and Impoverishment of the Country.

XXII. "With the exception," writes Consul CAMPBELL, of the 1910 reformed area, "of a few oases, which are frequent in the Kasai, but rare elsewhere, the 1910 area is practically exhausted (of rubber), and both the forest and the natives will require time to recover from the wholesale exploitation."[2] "An exhausted country must be given time to recover," he says elsewhere.[3] "Forest rubber is fast disappearing" —writes Consul ARMSTRONG of the 1912 unreformed area—"and by the time the Government surrenders its monopoly of this produce there will be none left."[4] Of that area he remarks further that by July 1912 it will have become "an impoverished country, containing no produce whatever."[5] Of sundry regions in the Kasai (1910 reformed area) Consul THURSTAN writes that "it is difficult to see how the majority of the natives" will be able to pay their complement of the silver

---

[1] Section II., paragraph V.
[2] p. 9 of the White Book.
[3] p. 13. of the White Book
[4] p. 20. of the White Book.
[5] p. 29. of the White Book.

taxes in future years. In the Maringa region (A.B.I.R.) Consul MACKIE notes the poverty of the natives and the Revs. WELCH, WHITESIDE and SKERRITT [1] corroborate the Consul's observations. Of Lake Leopold II. District (1911 reformed area) he speaks of the "forced collection" of rubber, which went on "for more than three years after it had been admitted that the forest was practically exhausted." Of the Equator District, as a whole, Consul MACKIE remarks that "the country is in a sadly exhausted state." [2]

XXIII. There is something peculiarly revolting and humiliating to those who agree with Mr. Asquith's definition of the national responsibilities of Great Britain, in the thought that the Belgian Government should be actually at the present moment prosecuting this process of exhaustion with the utmost vigour in any part of the Congo as is the case in the 1912 area; imposing an "ever-increasing rubber tax"; driving the wretched people to the forests for "twenty-one to twenty-five days in each month;" demanding "incesssant, ever-increasing and poorly-remunerated labour both for the supply of carriers and of food;" maintaining "in all its detail," a system, "similar to the state of affairs which existed under Congo Free State rule and which was condemned by the whole of the civilised world as slavery." [3]

The Scheme of Rubber Plantations: The Congo Reform Association's warnings in November, 1909.

XXIV. But the Association's principal desire at this stage in its analysis of the White Book is not so much to emphasise the disgraceful conditions still existing in the unreformed areas, as to point to the dangers which threaten the entire remaining population of the Congo owing to the future foreshadowed developments of Belgian policy. It seems almost inconceivable that the Belgian Government should contemplate further extensive demands upon native labour. But there are, the Association is reluctantly forced to acknowledge, reasons only too cogent to fear that this may be the case. In the Memorandum submitted to His Majesty's Government by the Association in November 1909, and to which allusion has already been made,[4] we deplored the announced resolve of the Belgian Government to inaugurate a new system of rubber plantations to be worked on Government account.[5] We pointed to the contradiction between this announced policy and enlightened European rule in other parts of tropical Africa, which seeks to encourage plantation work by European private enterprise, and by native communal enterprise. We expressed the hope that:

"the Secretary of State will also wish to assure himself that this scheme of "Government rubber plantations is not going to give an additional lease of "life to compulsory labour in another direction."

1 p. 80. of the White Book.
2 p. 87. of the White Book.
3 *Vide* Consul Armstrong's Report.
4 par. XV.
5 pp. 15 and 16 of the *Exposé de motifs*.

We asked how the labour demanded to clear and plant 5,000 acres (the figures contemplated by the Belgian Government) with rubber *per annum*, could possibly be obtained in the Congo without compulsion, when the population " required before everything a period of rest to recuperate." We asked whether the existing laws authorising compulsory labour for works of " public utility" such as the building of railways, would be invoked for the purpose of creating these Government rubber plantations. The Association is not aware whether these representations found any echo in Despatches to the Belgian Government from the Government of His Majesty, or in the course of conversations between His Majesty's Minister at Brussels and the Belgian Colonial Minister. Be that as it may, little has been heard of the project in Europe since it was first announced by the Belgian Government.

The testimony of the British Consular Staff. XXV. It transpires, however, from the White Book, that the Belgian Government seems determined to carry out its scheme, thus putting back the hands of the clock of modern conceptions of civilised duties in the African tropics. Consul CAMPBELL gives it as the view of the Authorities that " it is on plantations (of rubber) that the future of the country depends."[1] Elsewhere he speaks of the " considerable" demands for labour which will arise from the " establishment of rubber and other plantations." He adds significantly :

" The future depends to a great extent on private initiative ; and were the " Government by generous treatment to encourage companies and traders " with a moderate capital who will enrich the country, *instead of* " *exhausting it by the cultivation of rubber and other tropical* " *products* . . ."[2]

" The Government "—says Consul ARMSTRONG,[3] writing of the unopened areas— " hopes to be able to replace the wasted rubber forests with plantations. . . ." " It may, therefore, be concluded that the Government intends to devote its entire attention to rubber—to the exclusion of everything else."

Consul CAMPBELL recalls that the forced labour Decree of June 1906, was remodelled by that of February, 1910, and that under the latter, natives are still called upon to furnish labour, *under three years' contracts*, for works of " public utility." It is hardly necessary to state that no native of Africa will voluntarily contract for a three years' term of service. There seems to be no obstacle to this Decree being made to apply to Government rubber plantations since they are to be instituted for the purpose of raising revenue.

---

[1] p. 9 of the White Book.
[2] p. 13 of the White Book.
[3] p. 20 of the White Book.

XXVI. Thus a situation is plainly foreshadowed, when, coupled on the one hand with insecurity as to his inherent right of earning wealth and bettering his position by collecting and trading in the soil's products, and on the other hand, with handicaps upon commercial intercourse between Europeans and Natives, so onerous as to make the progressive development of trade highly questionable ; the native of the Congo, exhausted by long years of grinding oppression, is threatened with renewed calls upon his labour for a Government which, meantime, imposes upon him a tax in silver coin exceeding in the ratio of its incidence, taxes of a similar character levied in other tropical regions of Africa, happily spared the destructive processes of Congo Free State and Belgian rule.

The Native Army. XXVII. The last point the Association desires to bring to the notice of His Majesty's Government refers to the native army. It might have been supposed that the abrogation in a considerable part of the Congo of the system of exploitation and slavery, hitherto prevailing (a system requiring the constant use of military force) would have led to a considerable reduction in the native army. This reduction has not taken place, and in the unreformed regions the employment of armed ruffians, in addition to the regular troops, is vouched for by Consul ARMSTRONG. Consul MACKIE believes, indeed, that there is " every likelihood that the strength of the actual standing army will be reduced."[1] This belief is not borne out by the facts. The last official returns show the Belgian native army on the Congo to number 17,833 native ranks, and the contingent to be recruited this year was given at 3,375 men—whether an addition by that number to the above total, or replacing time-expired units, the Association is not informed. How disproportionate in numbers is this force, compared with area and population, to the military forces maintained by other Powers in the African tropics, the following Table will show :

	Area in sq. miles.	Population.	Military (native ranks).
British dependencies in Tropical Africa[2] —	928,535	26,026,790	9,489
German ditto[3] — —	574,209[5]	12,000,000[5]	3,828
French ditto[4] — —	2,255,090[5]	13,867,000[5]	12,416
The Congo under Belgian rule —	900,000	7,250,000	17,833

1 p. 88 White Book.
2 Nyassaland, Uganda, British East Africa, Northern Nigeria, Southern Nigeria, Gold Coast, Sierra Leone, Gambia.
3 Cameroons and German East Africa.
4 French West Africa and French Equatorial Africa.
5 The mileage and population here given do not take into account recent territorial changes, which increase both in the case of Germany, and decrease both, in the case of France, proportionately. *Vide* Sec. II. par. V.

What is the explanation?   **XXVIII.** While Great Britain requires under 10,000 native troops to keep order in a total area but very slightly larger than the Congo, inhabited by 26 million natives, many of them warlike and Mahommedans, Belgium requires nearly 18,000 Native troops to control 'a broken, impoverished, discouraged, Pagan population of 7¼ millions! France can manage nearly 14 million natives with 12,416 men, but Belgium requires 17,833 for a population half the size.

    XXIX. What is the explanation of so formidable a force? To this question the Association does not profess to suggest a reply. But, taken in conjunction with the traffic in arms so actively carried on by the Belgian Government,[1] precisely in one of the two portions of the Congo where more or less homogeneous native entities still survive, it is obvious that a situation is created replete with danger for the stability of European rule in the equatorial regions of the Dark Continent.

* * * * * * * * * * * * * * *

Belgian Obligations and Britain's Duty.   The cumulative effect of this consideration of facts relating to the future outlook of the Congo under Belgian rule, cannot, the Association believes, be impartially considered without grave anxiety. The Association is persuaded of the existence in Belgium of elements animated with the best of intentions. It has frequently rendered homage to the courageous, untiring, unceasing efforts of the distinguished Belgian statesman, M. EMILE VANDERVELDE, to improve the situation since annexation and to guide public opinion aright : and in many directions these efforts have succeeded in preventing reactionary measures and in checking abuses. But M. VANDERVELDE does not, unfortunately for the Congo, possess executive responsibility. On the other hand, the actions of the Belgian Government, and especially of the Belgian Colonial Minister, have not been such as to inspire confidence. By its policy the present Belgian Government is infringing International Treaty rights; disregarding the teaching of history, and falling short of the most essential requirements of civilised rule in tropical Africa.

    XXX. The Association submits that the "solemn obligations" of the British Government and people towards the native races of the Congo, proclaimed by Mr. ASQUITH, by leading statesmen of both Parties, by the House of Commons and by the religious leaders of the nation, are not fulfilled merely by refusing to grant

---

1 Section II., par VI.

the official·recognition of this country to Belgian rule in Africa, while a state of affairs such as that disclosed by the White Book prevails three years after the transfer of the Congo State to Belgium. Belgium, the Association holds, is rich enough to sweep away all existing abuses, and able, by legislative enactments, to place the future of the long persecuted Congo peoples upon a footing of permanent security. The Association. contends that if the words of the Prime Minister of Great Britain possess any real significance, it is the manifest duty of His Majesty's Government to insist upon the Belgian Government carrying out its Treaty obligations without further delay.

For the *CONGO REFORM ASSOCIATION,*

E. D. MOREL,

Honorary Secretary.

WHY THE FOREIGN OFFICE SAYS IT CANNOT MAKE OFFICIAL REPRESENTATIONS TO BELGIUM.

LETTER from the Foreign Office to The Congo Reform Association.

FOREIGN OFFICE,

December 30, 1911.

Sir,

I am directed by Secretary Sir E. GREY to acknowledge the receipt of your letter of the 5th inst. enclosing a Memorandum dealing with the Blue Book on the Congo question which has recently been laid before Parliament.

In your letter you specially draw Sir E. GREY's attention to two points:

(1.)—The maintenance of forced labour in the area not yet thrown open to freedom of trade.

(2.)—The Belgian Colonial Minister's recent utterances to His Majesty's Minister at Brussels.

With regard to (1) I am to state that His Majesty's Government have always been in agreement with the view taken by the Congo Reform Association as to the desirability of opening the whole of the Congo, including the 1912 zone, to freedom of trade at the earliest possible moment, and that the delay in recognising the Annexation of the Congo by Belgium has in a great measure been due to the policy adopted by the Belgian Government on this point.

With regard to (2) without discussing whether the Berlin Act referred to in your letter is the strongest ground on which one of its signatories, acting alone, could base action, I am to observe that for His Majesty's Government to make official representations to the Belgian Government would imply recognition of the annexation, a point that His Majesty's Government have been so far most careful to reserve. They have, however, not been the less active in bringing to the notice of the Belgian Government such facts as must receive attention before recognition is given.

I am, Sir,

Your most obedient, humble Servant,

(Signed)   W. LANGLEY.

E. D. Morel, Esq.;

Hon. Secretary of the Congo Reform Association,

"Granville House,"

Arundel Street, Strand, W.C..

THE ARGUMENT DEALT WITH.

SUGGESTION FOR AN INTERNATIONAL CONFERENCE.

LETTER from the Congo Reform Association to the Foreign Office.

January 2nd, 1912.

To the Right Hon. Sir EDWARD GREY, Bart., P.C., M.P.
> *His Majesty's Principal Secretary of State for Foreign Affairs,*
> > FOREIGN OFFICE, LONDON.

Sir,

I have the honour, on behalf of this Association to acknowledge receipt of your letter of December 30, 1911.

I note therefrom that His Majesty's Government have always been in agreement with the view taken by the Congo Reform Association as to the desirability of opening the whole of the Congo, including the 1912 zone, to freedom of trade at the earliest possible moment, and that the delay in recognising the annexation of the Congo by Belgium has in a great measure been due to the policy adopted by the Belgian Government on this point.

With regard to the language used to Sir FRANCIS VILLIERS, His Majesty's Minister at Brussels, by the Belgian Colonial Minister, amounting in effect to the contention that the internal condition of the Congo is a matter of exclusive Belgian concern, I note that without entering into a discussion as to the strongest selectable ground upon which to make official representations on the subject, His Majesty's Government are of opinion that any such official representations on their part would have the undesirable consequence of implying British recognition of the Belgium annexation.

The term "official representations" may have a technical significance with which the Association is not familiar; but I venture to point out that on January 7, 1909, and therefore some time after the annexa- of the Congo by Belgium, Sir ARTHUR HARDINGE, the then British Minister at Brussels, communicated officially with the Belgian Foreign Minister on the affairs of the Congo (*vide* Belgian Grey Book), and that on June 11 of the same year His Majesty's Government made an official communication to the Belgian Minister in London (C.D. 4701) on the affairs of the Congo. Neither of these official communications apparently implied a recognition of Belgian annexation on the part of His Majesty's Government.

While thanking the Secretary of State for his letter, which is confined to the two points raised in the letter from the Association covering its Memorandum on the Consular Reports, I venture to hope that the additional points raised in the Memorandum itself, and which may be summarised as under, will not have escaped the attention of His Majesty's Government :—

(1)—That the Reform Decrees restoring to the natives the right to gather and dispose of the fruits of their soil give no guarantee of permanence, seeing that this restoration is not acknowledged as an inherent right, but merely as a revocable concession from which the natives benefit " on sufferance."

(2)—That in the regions where these Reform Decrees have been applied freedom of trade is still handicapped and obstacles are systematically placed in the way of its development by the Belgian Government.

(3)—That in the regions where the Reform Decrees have not been applied the Belgian Government is conducting, contrary to International Law, an active traffic in arms in order to procure ivory, which traffic is denounced by the Consuls as a danger to the peace of all the neighbouring possessions.

(4)—That a renewal of forced labour in another form is threatened throughout the Congo, if the Belgian Government persists in its scheme of rubber plantations on Government account.

Since this Memorandum was despatched His Majesty's Government will doubtless have become acquainted with the contents of the Belgian Parliamentary paper containing the charges formulated by M. VANDERVELDE against the Belgian Administration and showing by official documents that forced labour for the construction of "public works" continues to prevail not only in the unreformed, but in the reformed areas.

To the Association it would not seem beyond the bounds of possibility for one of the great African Powers, sincerely desirous of vindicating the obligations contracted by Europe towards the Native Races of the Congo, to suggest a Conference, which should affect all the territories comprised within the conventional area as defined at Berlin in 1885. The recent exchange of territory which has taken place between France and Germany on the north bank of the Congo and within that area would seem in the Association's view to provide an excellent opportunity for a final settlement of the entire Congo question on the basis of the Berlin Act. The neglect of their obligations by the Powers in the past has resulted, *inter alia*, in an enormous, indeed an almost incredible, destruction of the native population, both in the Congo State and in the French Congo. The combined neglect of their obligations by the Powers in the future is bound in the nature of the case to lead to complications sooner or later. It would, the Association thinks, be a wise policy which should guard against them, as it would be a humane policy and a recognition, however tardy, of the responsibilities of the Western Powers towards the Native Races of the Congo Basin. The Association in recommending this suggestion desires to express its view that such proposals might well come with special appropriateness from His Majesty's Government.

I have the honour to be, Sir,

Your obedient Servant,

(Signed)　E. D. MOREL,

Hon. Secretary.

FOREIGN OFFICE REPLY TO THE SUGGESTION FOR AN INTERNATIONAL CONFERENCE.

LETTER from the Foreign Office to the Congo Reform Association.

FOREIGN OFFICE,

January 17th, 1912.

Sir,

I am directed by Secretary Sir E. GREY to acknowledge your letter of the 2nd instant drawing attention to the further points raised in the memorandum enclosed in your previous letter, and suggesting that His Majesty's Government should take the initiative in suggesting an International Conference for the settlement of the entire Congo question on the basis of the Berlin Act. I am to state that His Majesty's Government have no indication that a proposal for a Conference would meet with any more favourable reception than on previous occasions, whereas the desire of His Majesty's Government to co-operate in anything that would promote reform has been publicly expressed, and there can be no doubt on the part of any Power that shares these views that any proposal having this tendency would meet with a sympathetic response from His Majesty's Government.

I am to add that the points raised in the memorandum have not escaped attention.

I am, Sir,

Your most obedient, humble Servant,

(Signed) W. LANGLEY.

E. D. MOREL, Esq,

The Hon. Secretary, Congo Reform Association,

"GRANVILLE HOUSE,"

ARUNDEL STREET, STRAND.

FURTHER DISCUSSION ON THE SUGGESTION FOR AN INTERNATIONAL CONFERENCE.

LETTER from the Congo Reform Association to the Foreign Office.

February 5th, 1912.

To the Right Hon. Sir EDWARD GREY, Bart., P.C., M.P.,

His Majesty's Principal Secretary of State for Foreign Affairs,

FOREIGN OFFICE, LONDON.

Sir,

I have the honour, on behalf of this Association, to acknowledge receipt of the Secretary of State's letter of January 17th last.

This Association is glad to learn that His Majesty's Government are still desirous of co-operating in any measures that may seem generally advisable to regularise the state of affairs prevailing in the territories comprised within the Conventional Basin of the Congo; but that they have no indication leading them to suppose that a proposal coming from them would meet with a response more favourable than on previous occasions.

His Majesty's Government have, of course, greater facilities for judging of the latter point than the Association can have; but I would, nevertheless, make so bold as to recall that seven years have now elapsed since any formal suggestion of the nature referred to was put forward by His Majesty's Government. Many events have occurred in the interval, amongst others the entire accuracy of the reports of Sir ROGER CASEMENT and Lord CROMER, which formed the basis of the representations to the Powers of His Majesty's Government, has been established.

In a matter of this kind the Association assumes that success would depend very largely upon the method of approach, and that suggestions based upon the need of making the "open-door" for international commerce an effective reality throughout the Congo Basin, and for stopping the internationally illegal traffic in arms pursued by the Belgian Government (according to the reports of His Majesty's Consuls) might be better calculated to receive the influential support of such Powers as share the views of His Majesty's Government on these subjects, than suggestions bearing wholly upon problems of native treatment. As the preservation of the "open-door" for commerce, and all that it implies, is so potent a factor in securing just and normal administration of the native population in any tropical African territory, collective action in this regard could not fail in itself to remove many, if not most, of the undesirable features which the present situation continues to retain.

The Association does not, however, wish to press the matter at this stage beyond venturing to repeat that, in its view, a serious effort to ensure a return to practices consecrated by the Act of Berlin (practices in no way special or peculiar, since they prevail in tropical African territory not affected by that Act through the spontaneous recognition on the part of the responsible Powers of their indispensableness to good government) in the Conventional Basin of the Congo would be in the nature of a preventive to manifold difficulties which cannot fail to arise in the future if matters are left as they are, and which, in the nature of the case, would compel His Majesty's Government to intervene under circumstances possibly of greater complexity.

I have the honour to be, Sir,

Your obedient Servant,

(Signed) E. D. MOREL.

Hon. Secretary.

THE BELGIAN ADMINISTRATION'S TRAFFIC IN ARMS.

THE BELGIAN ADMINISTRATION'S TRAFFIC IN ARMS.

FOREIGN OFFICE,

February 21, 1912.

Sir,

I am directed by Secretary Sir E. GREY, to acknowledge the receipt of your letter of the 5th instant respecting the condition of affairs in the Congo.

Sir E. GREY notices that you refer in this letter, as in a previous communication, to "the internationally illegal traffic in arms pursued by the Belgian Government (according to the reports of His Majesty's Consuls)."

If you will refer to Vice-Consul ARMSTRONG's report, (page 30 of the Congo Blue Book, Africa No. 2, 1911), you will observe that, as far as this particular point is concerned, steps are being taken by the Belgian Government to remedy the evil.

I am, Sir,

Your most obedient, humble Servant,

(Signed)   W. LANGLEY.

E. D. MOREL, Esq.,

Hon. Secretary, the Congo Reform Association,

GRANVILLE HOUSE,

ARUNDEL STREET, STRAND.

THE BELGIAN ADMINISTRATION'S TRAFFIC IN ARMS.

GRANVILLE HOUSE,

ARUNDEL STREET,

STRAND, W.C.

February 23, 1912.

The Under-Secretary of State for Foreign Affairs.

FOREIGN OFFICE,

London. ·

Sir,

I have the honour to acknowledge receipt of your letter of February 21, in which the Secretary of State, recalling a passage in my letter of the 5th instant, where the ·—

"internationally illegal traffic in arms pursued by the Belgian "Government (according to the reports of His Majesty's Consuls)" is mentioned, refers to :—

"Vice-Consul ARMSTRONG's report (p. 30 of the Congo Blue Book, "Africa No. 2, 1911)."

Your letter states that a perusal of this document will show that :—

"as far as this point is concerned, steps are being taken by the Belgian "Government to remedy the evil."

In reply I beg to point out that the particular reference to which you draw my attention in Acting-Consul ARMSTRONG's report—in which this traffic is vehemently denounced—does not appear to the Association to be in any sense conclusive. The Consul does not, I may, perhaps, be pardoned for suggesting, say that "steps are being taken" by the Belgian Government. What he says is :—

"and *it is said* that henceforth no more arms and ammunition will be "furnished to the natives *except* by the order of a *high official*—a '*chef de* "*zone*' or a '*commissaire général.*'"

The Acting-Consul hardly conceals his own doubts on the subject, as will be observed by a reference to the sentence immediately following the above, and in the opening sentence of the third paragraph on the same page.

Moreover, the Acting-Consul says in another place (page 23) :—

"Payment is made in guns and ammunition . . . . etc."

Considering that it is the business of "high officials" in the Uelle District, to obtain rubber and ivory for revenue purposes from the natives ; that guns have for years past been the sole medium through which the Belgian Government has obtained ivory in that region ; that ivory from the Uelle District is still being collected and shipped from the Congo, the Association is unable to share the satisfaction of His Majesty's Government, although it would be pleased to hear that His Majesty's Government had received favourable reports of a later date than Acting-Consul ARMSTRONG's—written at the end of 1910. I venture to ask, on behalf of the Association, if such is the case, and, in that event, if these further reports can be laid before Parliament ?

The evil in question is a creation of the Belgian Government's predecessors. It has been perpetuated ever since annexation by the Belgian Administration. The Belgian Administration has admittedly obtained large sums by thus carrying on a traffic which is an offence against the the Law of Nations, and which as Acting-Consul ARMSTRONG remarks, is :—

"a positive menace to the tranquillity, not only of the Belgian Congo, but also of the neighbouring Colonies."

I have the honour to be, Sir,

Your obedient Servant,

(Signed)   E. D. MOREL,

Hon. Secretary.

P.S.—In connection with the difficulties placed by the Belgian Government in the way of legitimate trade, reported by His Majesty's Consuls, and as regards the fears they express in the last reports issued by His Majesty's Government, it may possibly be of interest to the Secretary of State if I give below an extract from a public lecture (which may conceivably have escaped the Secretary of State's notice) delivered this month by Professor Hans Meyer before the Berlin Geographical Society. Professor Hans Meyer has recently returned from a visit to German East Africa, having penetrated westwards as far as the Congo Border. In the course of his remarks, the Professor said:—

"The Congo State, having for a short time during 1910 shown itself more compliant, has again begun to obstruct commerce with German territory in the highest degree. It has again monopolised ivory and rubber and confiscated the rubber stores purchased by German merchants, thereby ruining many of them. Complaints have had no effect. There is an embargo on the trade with rubber and ivory, and the goods which come from thence into our free trade zone are smuggled. German trade, however, can only flourish if Belgium gives up her policy of monopolization and at last introduces the free trade which it promised when the Congo State was first established. For this reason a new Congo Conference is neccessary."

The selling of arms and ammunition to native rulers for the acquisition of rubber and ivory; interference with international trade; forced labour for every form of Government work (including gold-mining, exploited as a Government monopoly), combined with the presence of 18,000 native soldiers living on the country—these things, amongst others, in the Association's opinion, are so many elements which foreshadow, sooner or later, grave disturbances over a large Central African field, if the Governments concerned in upholding the Act of Berlin take no steps to deal with them.

E. D. M.